D1362363

Notable Americans

FIRST LADY:
The Story of
Hillary Rodham Clinton

Aaron Boyd

MORGAN
REYNOLDS
Incorporated

Greensboro

FIRST LADY: *The Story of Hillary Rodham Clinton*

Library of Congress Cataloging-in-Publication Data
Boyd, Aaron, 1955-
    First Lady : the story of Hillary Rodham Clinton / Aaron Boyd. -- 1st ed.
        p.   cm. -- (Notable Americans)
    Includes bibliographical references and index.
    ISBN 1-883846-02-1 (cloth)
    1. Clinton, Hillary Rodham —Juvenile literature. 2. Presidents'
spouses—United States—Biography—Juvenile literature. 3. Clinton,
Bill, 1946- --Juvenile literature. [1. Clinton, Hillary Rodham.
2. First ladies. 3. Clinton, Bill, 1946- .] I. Title.
II. Series.
E887.C55B68 1994
973.929' 092 -- dc20
[B]

                                                        93-21195
                                                            CIP
                                                            AC

Cover photo courtesy of AP/Wide World

Printed in the United States of America

First Edition

5 4 3 2 1

To Anita

CONTENTS

PARK RIDGE

1992, designated by some as the Year of the Woman, was a watershed year in American politics. Carol Moseley Braun surprised the experts by defeating long-time Democratic incumbent Senator Alan Dixon, and went on to become the first female, African-American senator in American history. In the state of Washington, Patty Murray, a self described "mom in tennis shoes," won election to the U.S. Senate; and California, the most populous state, elected two women senators, Diane Feinstein and Barbara Boxer. That year saw more women elected, or appointed, to political office than ever before.

As 1992 continued into 1993, the most visible, and controversial, of the new women political leaders was clearly Hillary Rodham Clinton, wife of Bill Clinton, the 42nd President of the United States.

Hillary Rodham Clinton is different from any previous First Lady. She is the first presidential wife born after World War II, part of what is known as the baby-boom generation, and the first whose political and social philosophy was formed in the difficult but idealistic era of the Vietnam War, the African-American civil rights movement, and the women's rights movement.

A graduate of Yale Law School who has forged a career as a powerful and influential lawyer, she is definitely a highly intelligent and capable person in her own right, with numerous special achievements apart from those of her husband. But her role as Bill Clinton's chief political and policy advisor is by far the most controversial aspect of Hillary's career. She is in charge of the Clinton Administration's effort to fix the nation's health care system, perhaps the most massive attempt at governmental reform since the New Deal of the 1930s. Almost certainly, she will oversee the administration's attempt to overhaul the country's welfare system.

Hillary Rodham Clinton is a new type of American political leader. Perhaps in the future we will be able to look back and see her career as a critical step in the progression toward the election of a woman as president.

But, what about the woman herself? What combination of social forces and private influences have helped to create this powerful and controversial First Lady?

***

During the 1992 presidential campaign, Hillary explained why she had devoted so much of her career toward improving the lives of children. "I was raised to believe that I had obligations because I was a blessed person," she answered. "To whom much is given, much is expected."

The source of many of these blessings is her parents, who devoted themselves to providing their children with the best possible opportunities in life.

Hugh Rodham, Hillary's father, had come a long way during his life. He attended Penn State University on a football scholarship, but graduated in the middle of the Depression, when millions of people could not find jobs. Hugh was forced to perform physical labor in the coal mines of western Penn-sylvania before he found a job as a salesman for Columbia Lace Company, a Chicago drapery manu-facturer. Here he would begin a long and successful career, and meet his future wife, Dorothy Howell, a young secretary from California, when she ap-plied for a job at Columbia Lace. He and Dorothy were married in 1942.

After military service during World War II, Hugh started his own drapery manufacturing business. He worked long hours, and it was not long before he turned the business into a profitable company.

Hillary Diane Rodham, born in Chicago on October 26, 1947, was Hugh and Dorothy's first child. When she was three, the family moved from Chicago to Park Ridge, a suburb north of the city, where Hillary's two younger brothers, Hugh Jr. and Tony, were born. Park Ridge was and is a peaceful place to raise a family, and although the Rodhams were not wealthy, their new home in Park Ridge was large enough to comfortably contain the grow-ing family.

In many ways, the Rodhams were a typical 1950s family. Dorothy worked as a homemaker, while Hugh commuted to Chicago to run the growing drapery business. The family attended a nearby Methodist Church on Sundays, and neighborhood children played together on the peaceful, tree-lined streets. "There must have been forty or fifty children within a four-block radius of our house," Dorothy Rodham remembers. "Hillary held her own at cops and robbers, hide and seek, chase and run—all the games that children don't play anymore."

Hillary soon learned to stand up for herself. Shortly after the Rodhams moved to Park Ridge, a neighborhood girl began picking on the newcomer. Hillary, who had no experience with bullies, burst into tears and ran home. Dorothy explained to her daughter that she could either be afraid of the girl and suffer her taunts, or stand up to her. It was difficult for Hillary to accept this advice, and for a while she allowed the girl to continue harassing her. Then one day, while the other children looked on, the girl pushed Hillary to the sidewalk and kicked her. After a moment of listening to the laughing onlookers, Hillary stood up and charged the surprised bully, driving her down the street.

Hugh Rodham Sr., though loving and supportive of his daughter, was a tougher taskmaster than Mrs. Rodham. He felt his children could always achieve more by trying harder, and consequently set very high standards for his daughter, especially in school.

As Hillary remembers, "I would come home from school with a good grade, and my father would say, 'Must have been an easy assignment.'"

Hillary did try harder, and soon discovered she was a natural leader. She organized games and activities, including a neighborhood circus. "Mothers in the neighborhood were amazed at how they couldn't get their boys to do much, but Hillary had them all running around," Dorothy remembers.

Dorothy and Hugh made every attempt to instill the right values and beliefs in their children. And if the Rodhams believed in anything, it was in the best possible education for their children. Dorothy did not have a college degree; though she enjoyed her life as a homemaker, she sometimes felt uncomfortable talking at social gatherings because of her lack of formal higher education. She wanted more for her daughter; Hillary should never feel inadequate or inferior. The more practical Hugh saw education as the key to social and financial success. From an early age Hillary knew, "I had an obligation to use my mind. They told me that an education would enable me to have a lot more opportunities in life. It was education for education's sake, but also it was the idea that school was a pathway to a better opportunity."

One of Hillary's first lessons, imparted by her mother, was that success and the realization of dreams was not confined to men. "There was no distinction between me and my brother, or any barriers thrown up to me that I couldn't think about doing something because I was a girl," she remembers. "It was just: if you work hard enough and you really apply yourself, then you should be able to do whatever you choose to do."

Fortunately, Park Ridge had an excellent public school system. Beginning in elementary school, Hillary made high grades. Reading and writing came easily to her, but she worked even harder on her arithmetic. Outside of school, Hillary participated in Girl Scouts, earning every possible merit badge. She approached each challenge with the same energetic determination. As her brother Hugh remembers, "Hillary was always very focused." Hillary's parents later admitted to being "slightly uncomfortable" at Hillary's concentrated over-achievement.

Sometimes, though, even hard work and determination were not enough. Although Hillary studied piano for years, she was never able to play a melody with more than one hand. She loved dance classes, but had little talent for the more difficult ballet stances.

In October 1957, when the Soviet Union launched Sputnik, the first rocket to successfully orbit the earth, Americans became aware of how important science education was to the country's future. During this period, Hillary decided on a career as an astronaut. She wrote a letter to NASA, the agency in charge of America's space program, and requested information on preparing for a career in space. But a NASA official wrote back that there was nothing she could do—in that era, women were barred from becoming astronauts. Hillary was angry and disappointed. She was an excellent student, capable of learning the necessary math and science skills. She had never allowed her gender to stop her from achieving her goals, including playing forward on the field hockey team. Now she was being denied an opportunity, not because she was unqualified, but simply because she was a girl.

Later, as she entered Main East High School, Hillary noticed that many of her girl friends, who had earned excellent grades in the lower levels, began holding themselves back, attempting to appear less intelligent than they really were. They thought boys would be intimidated by "smart girls," and would not ask them out on dates. Other girls took less demanding courses so they could be in the same classes as their boyfriends. Hillary could not understand why her friends would limit themselves in this way. She was so determined not to let her social life interfere with her school work that when her mom suggested she wear makeup, at first Hillary refused. "She didn't have time for it," Dorothy remembers.

Hillary had plenty of male friends. Although she did not overly concern herself with appearance, she was attractive, with blond hair and bright blue eyes. She was also cheerful, quick to laugh, and eager to be social—but only when she had the time. Her brother Tony, who sometimes found it difficult to live in his older sister's shadow, remembers that, "When she wasn't studying, she was a lot of fun."

Hillary's social life in high school was similar to that of other teenagers all over the country during the early 1960s. She went to school dances and sports events, urging the football and basketball teams toward victory; she spent leisure time hanging out with her friends, drinking cokes or milkshakes and talking. She was part of a large circle of kids from her neighborhood and adjoining ones. A dozen or so of the group would get together, often at her friend Betsy Johnson's house, where they spent afternoons watching favorite television shows, discussing the latest school gossip or movies and record albums, and occasionally pigging out on junk food. It was a normal, happy adolescence, occurring before the vast social and cultural changes that would make the late 1960s so turbulent and confusing for young people. Recreational drugs were almost unheard of, and Hillary never felt the need or the desire to experiment with alcohol. Although she occasionally dated, much of her social life revolved around group outings. One acquaintance, Steve Goodman, would achieve fame as a folk singer and songwriter, whose song "City of New Orleans" would become a classic before his early death from leukemia.

Hillary kept busy both in school and out. She organized the school's annual talent shows. She was named head of the committee which arranged and scheduled the student assemblies, which, at a school with an enrollment exceeding 2500, was a formidable task. As a junior at Main East High School, she was elected vice president of her class.

Her hard work, first at Main East, and then during her senior year at Main South High School, paid off with a bevy of honors and awards as she neared graduation. At Main South, she was appointed a "senior leader," and assisted the faculty with various class instructional duties. Her high grades qualified her to be a member of the National Honor

Society, and she won the Good Citizen Award from the Daughters of the American Revolution. To top it off, her senior class voted her as "Most Likely To Succeed," one instance in which a yearbook prophecy certainly came true. Hillary was such a standout that one teacher still recalls where she sat in his classroom. "In the fifth row, in the seventh seat," he remembers. Another teacher recalls her as "bright, articulate, a young lady of conviction."

Hillary's teenage years were not totally devoted to school and extracurricular activities, however. Her parents also encouraged her to earn her own spending money. She worked part-time in a day care center, and baby-sat for younger children in the neighborhood. Later, she worked as a store clerk, and had a summer job maintaining the sports equipment in a public park.

Church was important to the Rodham family. They attended the First United Methodist Church every Sunday. The Methodist Church stressed the teachings of founder John Wesley, who believed that it was as important for a Christian to be as concerned with doing good in the world as she was about her own salvation. Don Jones, fresh out of Drew University, where he had been a student of the progressive thinking theologian and author

Paul Tillich, became youth minister at First United Methodist. He was to become a strong influence on Hillary and on many of her friends, introducing them to new ways of thinking about their social duties as Christians. He used art and popular culture—the socially-conscious songs of Bob Dylan, the poetry of e.e. cummings, paintings by Picasso —to introduce his largely upper-middle class students to the world outside affluent Park Ridge. "He was just relentless in telling us that to be a Christian did not just mean you were concerned about your personal salvation," Hillary remembers.

Reverend Jones helped form many of Hillary's views toward public service and helping the less fortunate. He was also responsible for one of the most exciting events of her adolescence when, in 1962, he took his church youth group into Chicago to hear the Reverend Dr. Martin Luther King Jr. give a speech. After the address, Hillary's group was ushered backstage, where Hillary felt honored to shake Dr. King's hand.

The youth group also made trips to the inner city of Chicago, where they helped other organizations working with the urban poor. Hillary even organized a group of volunteers, including several neighborhood boys, who baby-sat for the children of migrant laborers while the parents worked.

Hillary had always considered herself to be a Republican, like her father. In 1964, her senior year of high school, she worked as a "Goldwater Girl," a teenage volunteer on Republican Barry Goldwater's campaign for president. Later, her political affiliation would change, but at the time Hillary was happy to follow her parent's lead.

As high school drew to a close, Hillary began thinking of college. She graduated from an excellent high school in the top five percent of her class, and could take her pick of the best universities in the country. Many of her friends chose to attend local schools, such as the University of Chicago, but Hillary wanted to go farther away. She was eager to see the world beyond Park Ridge. After discussing it with her parents, she decided to apply to both Smith and Wellesley. Both were small, prestigious women's colleges; an education at either would prepare her for a successful career in any field she chose.

Both schools accepted her, and she was faced with a difficult decision. When asked later why she had decided on Wellesley, Hillary admitted she still did not know. "It just felt right," she said. As she prepared to leave for Massachusetts in the fall of

1965, she of course felt some sadness about leaving Park Ridge. It had been a comfortable, secure place in which to grow up. But she was also eager to move on to the next stage of her life.

WELLESLEY

Hillary had only seen photographs of Wellesley College before arriving to begin classes, but she was not disappointed. Located on the outskirts of Boston, Massachusetts, the campus' Gothic stone buildings, tall trees, and well-tended lake matched Hillary's ideal of a tradition-steeped institution. She soon discovered that many of Wellesley's rules were old-fashioned as well. First-year students could not have a car, entertain boys in their rooms, or leave campus on the weekend without written parental permission. Most social activities consisted of chaperoned dances, afternoon teas, and sporting events.

Some classmates at Wellesley were the daughters of America's most wealthy and influential families. Hillary's best friend throughout college, Eldee Acheson, was the granddaughter of Dean

Acheson, President Harry Truman's Secretary of State. Another classmate was the daughter of Paul Nitze, Deputy Secretary of Defense in the Kennedy and Johnson administrations and later Chief Arms Negotiator for President Ronald Reagan. This was heady company for a girl from Park Ridge, and years later Hillary admitted to being slightly overwhelmed at first. But she soon overcame her shyness, and her room in Stone-Davis dormitory became the main gathering place for a wide circle of friends.

During her first year, Hillary dated Harvard junior Jeff Shields, who remembers her as a lively companion, interested in learning new things. "She listened to what people were thinking about and were interested in reading, and then she'd read that author's work and come back and be able to discuss it. It was a relationship based on a lot of discourse." Their dates usually consisted of walks around the campus, football games, and parties, where Hillary often danced for hours to the music of her favorite music group, The Supremes, and other popular artists.

When she first arrived at Wellesley, Hillary had looked much as she had in Park Ridge. Despite her mother's admonitions, she still cared little about her clothes, wore thick glasses, and spent little time styling her hair. Her attire usually consisted of "Peter Pan" blouses and pleated skirts.

However, Hillary's dress soon changed. The thick eye wear gave way to "granny glasses," similar to those made popular by the late Beatle John Lennon, and the skirt-and-blouse outfits were replaced by long "peasant" dresses or jeans.

Her politics also changed during these years. When Hillary arrived at Wellesley, she believed in the type of individual public service she had learned from her church elders and high school teachers, but thought governmental action could do little to improve people's lives. But her experiences at college, both inside and outside the classroom, were quickly to alter her political philosophy toward more "liberal" ideas.

Hillary majored in political science; the professor who most influenced her was Alan Schechter, who taught Constitutional Law. Schechter's main interest was civil rights, which he saw as a moral, as well as a political, issue. Schechter knew most of his students had come from privileged, secure backgrounds, and he attempted to make them aware of how less fortunate people lived. In many ways, Professor Schechter assumed the mentor role toward Hillary that Reverend Jones had served in

Park Ridge. Schechter remembers Hillary as "the best student I had taught in the first seven years I taught at Wellesley. She had strong analytical abilities. She could look at a problem objectively, and as a researcher, she was very thorough and detailed."

Much of the change in Hillary's political views would result from events occurring in America during her college tenure. Her four years at Wellesley, 1965-69, were among the most turbulent in American history. The Vietnam War escalated, and increasing numbers of people publicly opposed the conflict. In January of 1968, the North Vietnamese launched a strike deep into South Vietnam that became known as the Tet Offensive, and American television networks carried live images of the United States Embassy in Saigon, coming under fierce attack. In April of 1968, civil rights leader Martin Luther King Jr. was killed in Memphis, Tennessee, an event which sparked widespread riots and racial turmoil. Then, on June 5, 1968, Senator Robert Kennedy was assassinated in Los Angeles while campaigning for the Democratic Party's presidential nomination. When the Democratic Convention met in Chicago later that summer to nominate Hubert Humphrey for President, the streets outside the convention hall were alive with protestors. Chicago police used brutal tactics to control the demonstrators, most of whom were young college students.

Hillary, home for the summer, went into Chicago with a childhood friend during the Democratic Convention and personally witnessed the violence. "We saw kids our age getting their heads beaten in," the friend recalls. "And the police were doing the beating. Hillary and I just looked at each other. We had had a wonderful childhood in Park Ridge, but we obviously hadn't gotten the whole story."

During this period, many Americans changed their attitudes toward the role of government in America, and toward the nature of society in general. This change was most obvious on college campuses. Students organized anti-war protests. Black students demanded equal opportunities for education, jobs and housing. And, especially at schools like Wellesley, women began asking why historically they had been denied leadership roles in much of American life.

The late 1960s was an exciting time to be a college student. It could also be a dangerous time. As the youth movements continued, drugs became more common, and many young people were swept up in their destructive allure. For example, one student who had been voted "Most Likely To Succeed" at Main East High School died of a drug overdose in 1969. A young person needed skill and intelligence to navigate the rapid social changes.

But Hillary flourished in the way the people who had known her in Park Ridge would have expected. Students were attracted by her sense of humor, her friendliness, and her ability to make everyone feel valuable. "She was a down-to-earth person, she had a great sense of humor, and people liked her," one Wellesley classmate remembers.

Hillary and her friends were concerned with the political and social issues of the day. They agreed that American society and its political parties should better reflect the changes going on around them. But they were not "radicals", wishing to tear down the existing social order. Instead, they discussed ways to make government more responsive to people's needs. One group member recalls, "I would describe us all as typically earnest students of the late sixties: idealists, thinking that maybe one person could make a difference."

Hillary's leadership role did not overly inflate her ego. She and Eldee Acheson had many conversations about politics and public policy, both in and out of the classroom. "She was not one of those know-it-alls who lectured people and lectured the professor and answered everything in the context of their political beliefs," Eldee remembers.

Hillary wanted to test her knowledge and ideas against the reality of the world around her. As her understanding increased of how people outside of the suburbs lived, and as she became more knowledgeable about controversial issues, she became less conservative politically. She no longer thought poverty could be ended without government help; or that women and minorities would be treated equally until further laws against discrimination were enacted. And she became convinced that the U.S. should withdraw from Vietnam. She was no longer the "Goldwater Girl" who had first arrived at Wellesley.

However, Hillary never lost confidence in the American system of government. Unlike more militant students, she did not advocate violent revolution or radical change. Hillary's political beliefs changed from the conventional Republican ideas of her father, to the conventional Democratic ideas reflected in her friend Eldee Acheson. She was never anti-American, and she never lost her faith in the religion she had learned as a child.

Hillary maintained a busy schedule during her four years at Wellesley. She volunteered to work in Roxbury, a Boston inner city neighborhood, as a reading tutor. She participated in student government.

Hillary also demonstrated her skill as a mediator in a dramatic way. When African-American students became convinced that Wellesley was using a secret quota system to keep black enrollment down, they threatened a student strike. Hillary led the effort to reach an agreement between the administration and the black students. She moderated a meeting held in the campus chapel, and made sure both sides in the developing conflict got a fair hearing. Eventually, an agreement was reached, and the student strike was avoided.

In 1968, Hillary showed her increased political consciousness by working as a volunteer on Senator Eugene McCarthy's campaign for the Democratic presidential nomination. When McCarthy, who campaigned on a platform to end the war, lost the nomination to Hubert Humphrey, Hillary and her friend Eldee Acheson continued to support the Democrats over the Republicans, who nominated Richard Nixon. In the general election campaign, the pair called voters and distributed Humphrey campaign literature. Although Humphrey lost the race in one of the closest elections in history, Hillary enjoyed her first taste of electoral politics.

Hillary's senior year was the culmination of a highly successful college career. She served as president of the student government, and used her post to organize a campus wide teach-in about the war in Vietnam. She participated on the nation-wide television show *College Bowl*, a popular show of the era that pitted teams from different colleges in quiz competition. The teams were composed of four players, and the emphasis was on answering highly detailed questions, drawn from several academic disciplines, in a short amount of time. The Wellesley team won multiple rounds, largely due to Hillary's participation, and her success brought her a great deal of publicity. Her senior thesis, entitled "Aspects of the War on Poverty," earned a perfect score, and guaranteed she would graduate with honors. As commencement day approached, Hillary was the most respected student on campus.

Several of the students of Hillary's class of 1969 decided that, for the first time ever, a graduating student should be allowed to speak at the commencement ceremony. This was an attitude characteristic of the time, when students all over the country were impatient to be heard. But for conservative Wellesley it was a radical idea, and the college president, Ruth Adams, refused the students' request.

The young women, including Hillary, were not to be deterred. When the student government, and the entire student body, let it be known they supported the idea, the group began deciding on a speaker. If they could approach the president with the name of a highly respected student, someone trusted by both the students and the administration, they were more likely to receive approval.

Hillary was their first choice for speaker, and she accepted the honor. When the students re-approached the college president with their suggestion, Adams agreed—with conditions. The speech could not be embarrassing, or reflect badly on the school. Also, it should not be Hillary's personal speech, but should attempt to speak to the entire class.

A team of students worked on the speech for days. They wanted it to summarize their last four years, while also voicing their dreams and aspirations for the future. When the team finished its work, Hillary added her comments.

The guest speaker for the 1969 Wellesley commencement was Massachusetts Senator Edward

Brooke. Brooke, a Republican, was the first African-American Senator since Reconstruction, the era immediately following the Civil War.

Senator Brooke spoke first. Most present that day remember little about his speech, except that it was vague. Eldee Acheson recalls, "It was pretty much a canned speech, full of highfalutin´ words and concepts. He did not weave into its ideas or its content or its message anything about the four years we had spent at that school and what had happened to the country in those four years." It was clearly not a speech to satisfy the impatient, activist students of the Wellesley class of 1969.

After the polite applause that followed the Senator's words, Hillary approached the podium. She looked small in her bulky black gown and wide mortar board—until she began speaking. "I find myself in a familiar position," she began, "that of reacting, something that our generation has been doing for quite a while now."

Much to the audiences' surprise, Hillary diverted from the prepared text. "I find myself reacting just briefly to some of the things that Senator Brooke said. This has to be brief because I do have a little speech to give," she continued. She went on to say that the Senator's remarks reflected what was wrong with his generation. Her generation wanted relevancy, a politics of the "impossible made possible." Senator Brooke, and others like him, offered only empathy, and "empathy doesn't do us anything. We've had lots of empathy; we've had lots of sympathy." After criticizing Senator Brooke, Hillary launched into the long speech she and the other students had written. But she had already made her impression. "Some people, largely mothers, thought it was just rude and never got off that point," Eldee Acheson recalls, referring to the rebuke of Brooke. "And another group thought she was absolutely right. It distracted a lot of people."

Hillary's address was featured in *Life* magazine, along with a photo of her dressed in brightly striped pants, balloon-sleeved shirt, sandals, and wire framed glasses. Her college experience had changed her; she was no longer the bobby-socked girl from Park Ridge. It had been an intense four years, but there would be more changes in her future, including an encounter with a Rhodes Scholar from Arkansas named Bill Clinton.

LAW SCHOOL

As far back as high school, Hillary's friends had believed her interests in government and public policy would prod her to attend law school. One classmate remembers, "You looked at Hillary and you knew she wanted to be a lawyer, she was going to be a lawyer." Now, it was time to do just that. Hillary's academic success at Wellesley allowed her to choose from the nation's best law schools.

She quickly narrowed her choices to Harvard and Yale Universities. Both contained top law schools. She made her final decision only when a friend, who wanted her to choose Harvard, introduced her to a law professor from that institution. Hillary began questioning him about the school. But the professor interrupted Hillary and said: "We don't need any more women." As Hillary remembered later, "That's what made my decision. I was leaning toward Yale anyway, but that fellow's comments iced the cake."

Yale University, located in New Haven, Connecticut, is one of the most prestigious schools in the country, and counts among its alumni many of the country's past and present leaders, including former President George Bush. A law degree from Yale would be a great advantage to any career Hillary chose. But Hillary had not yet decided on a career. She knew she wanted a law degree, but had not determined what she wanted to do after that.

The heated politics of the 1960s continued during Hillary's years at Yale. New Haven, although the home of one of America's premier universities, is also an industrial city with great ethnic diversity. Shortly after Hillary arrived, a politically controversial trial began in a courthouse near the campus. The trial involved the murder trial of Erica Huggins and Bobby Seale, two leaders of the Black Panthers, a militant African-American group with radical politics. Many Black Panther supporters believed the two were arrested on false charges because they were leaders of a revolutionary group. Tension was high, and the conflict spilled over onto the Yale campus, where a suspicious fire broke out in the law library, and a student demonstration had to be broken up by police with tear gas. A group of law students demanded their fellow students hold a strike, or even seize physical control of the law school. Hillary did not want the school to be closed, and was determined to do what she could to keep that from happening.

As angry student activists filled an auditorium and began making rousing speeches to the crowd, Hillary sat quietly on the stage and listened intently to what was said. At the completion of each speech, Hillary asked the speaker questions, to make sure everyone understood what had been said. As the speeches continued, Hillary led the group in discussing ways they could make their unhappiness with the Yale administrators known without closing the law school. It was a remarkable achievement for a first year law student. "We no longer remember what the meeting was about—we can only remember we were awed by her," one classmate said years later. By the end of her first year at Yale, Hillary was as respected as she had been at Wellesley.

It was also during her first year that Hillary decided on the direction she wanted her law career to take. One day, while reading the notices on a bulletin board, she saw an announcement for an upcoming speech by Marion Wright Edelman.

Marion was the wife of Peter Edelman, the director of a League of Women Voters conference Hillary had attended the previous summer. Hillary attended the talk, where Ms. Edelman spoke about her work in the area of children's rights. Hillary was intrigued by the ideas put forth. After the speech, she asked Ms. Edelman if she could work with her in Washington, D.C., during the summer, and Ms. Edelman agreed.

Hillary spent the next summer working on Capitol Hill, where as part of her job, she interviewed working parents and their children. This experience convinced her that there was a great deal that could be done to improve the lives of America's children. Hillary, who had organized a baby-sitting service for migrant workers' children back in high school, decided to devote her law career to improving children's lives. When she returned to Yale for her second year, she began taking courses on children and the law. She also worked at the Yale Child Studies Center, and later collaborated with two professors on books about the role of children in the legal and educational systems.

Hillary's reputation among her fellow law students grew quickly. She was a formidable presence, someone who was highly intelligent, disciplined,

Hillary, in typical counter-culture attire, while being interviewed for *Life* magazine after her controversial speech at the Wellesley graduation ceremonies in 1969. (Lee Balterman/*Life* magazine)

Hillary Rodham looks on as her husband answers questions from the media during Bill Clinton's first term as Governor of Arkansas. (AP/Wide World Photos)

and obviously destined for success. Another student had a similar reputation for high achievement. Bill Clinton was older than most of the other students, because he had spent two years studying in Oxford, England, as a Rhodes Scholar. The Rhodes Scholarship is considered the highest honor that can be given to a graduating college senior. But Bill, besides being a good student, was tall and handsome, and a witty conversationalist.

Hillary has often told the story of how she first noticed Bill Clinton. One afternoon, while walking through the student lounge with a friend, she heard a man say: "And not only that, we grow the biggest watermelons in the world."

Hillary asked about the young man. "That's Bill Clinton," her friend said. "He's from Arkansas. That's all he ever talks about."

Hillary noticed Bill was attractive, as well as a loud talker, but went on her way. Then, studying in the library a few days later, she noticed Bill talking with a student. Bill was looking at her. Hillary began looking back. Finally, Hillary stood up and walked over to Bill and said: "Look, if you're going to keep staring at me and I'm going to keep staring back, we should at least introduce ourselves. I'm Hillary Rodham. What's your name?"

Bill was so surprised at her forwardness that he

literally could not remember his own name. But he was soon able to get over his surprise. Within a few weeks, the couple began dating.

Although Hillary and Bill were similar in many ways, their respective childhoods had taken somewhat different paths. When Bill was born, on August 19, 1946, his mother was already a widow. Bill's father, William Jefferson Blythe III, died in a car wreck four months before Bill was born. As a young child, Bill lived with his maternal grandparents in Hope, Arkansas, while his mother studied nursing in New Orleans. He loved his grandparents, but the separation from his mother was painful.

When Bill was four she returned to Hope and married a car dealer, Roger Clinton. Later, the family moved to Hot Springs, Arkansas, where Bill's younger brother, Roger Jr., was born. Roger Clinton Sr. later adopted Bill, and he changed his name to William Jefferson Clinton.

Bill Clinton was a brilliant student, excelling in his school work and in the high school band, where he played the tenor saxophone. Popular and outgoing, he was so involved in school politics that his principal had to forbid him from holding any more offices.

Although outwardly happy, life in the Clinton

house was not always pleasant. Roger Clinton was an alcoholic, and often became abusive. Bill witnessed drunken rages, including physical attacks on his mother. However, even with these problems, Bill graduated at the top of his high school class, and won a partial scholarship to Georgetown University in Washington, D.C. While at Georgetown, Bill earned excellent grades, worked part-time in Arkansas Senator William Fulbright's Capitol Hill office, and participated in student politics. His time at Georgetown was as active as Hillary's years at Wellesley.

As graduation approached, Bill was awarded the Rhodes Scholarship. While at Oxford, Bill studied government and philosophy, and traveled around Europe. After two years at Oxford, Bill accepted a scholarship to study law at Yale.

Although Bill had many friends, there was something about Hillary Rodham that made her stand out from the rest. "I could just look at her and tell she was interesting and deep," he said later. After only a few dates, Hillary and Bill became steady companions. They attended parties together, dancing late into the night, or listening to music by Judy Collins, The Rolling Stones, and other contemporary groups.

Bill did not live in a dormitory at Yale, but shared

a house with three other students at nearby Fort Trumball Beach. Hillary soon became a regular guest at the house. The friends played volleyball on the beach, and shared pot luck dinners; evenings were often spent discussing the issues of the day. "It was one large philosophical discussion," is how one friend remembers the conversations.

Hillary and Bill seemed made for each other. "They were a dynamic couple," Bill's roommate William Coleman remembers. But, as he admitted later, Bill was worried about becoming romantically involved with Hillary because of their different career plans. Bill was determined to return home and pursue a political career. "I've got to go home to Arkansas," he said. "It's just who I am."

Hillary knew little about Arkansas, but it was not where she had planned to live. Her plans centered on either Washington or New York City. Arkansas seemed like a place near the end of the earth.

The young couple did not let the future distract them from making the most of their time together at Yale. They competed as a team in a "mock" trial, held to help train law students to argue cases before a judge and jury. Although they approached the project with their typical zest and determination, they failed to win the competition. Bill joked they lost because Hillary wore a bright red dress which distracted the judge's attention.

In the fall of 1972, the couple took time away from classes to travel to Texas to work for the campaign of George McGovern, the Democratic nominee for president. McGovern's chief issue was ending the Vietnam War, and he won the support of millions of young people tired of the long conflict. Both Bill and Hillary were enthusiastic McGovern supporters. Hillary registered voters near the Texas-Mexico border, and Bill worked in the Austin headquarters. Although McGovern lost in a landslide to Richard Nixon in the November election, Hillary made several close friends during the campaign. One was Betsey Wright, who would later work for Bill when he became governor of Arkansas.

Bill visited Hillary's parents over the Christmas break of 1972. At first, the Rodham family was unsure what they thought about the extroverted young man from Arkansas. But before the week was out, they had been charmed by his warmth and enthusiasm. However, the Rodhams did not want Hillary to move to Arkansas. In the spring, Hillary paid a visit to Bill's family. She later admitted that before the visit she had believed the state was populated by hillbillies spitting tobacco juice out of pickup trucks. Instead, she discovered it was a beautiful state, and that the people were warm and friendly. However, she still did not want to live in a rural southern state.

Back at Yale, Hillary did not allow her active life, and her romance with Bill, to distract her from her studies. She remained at the top of her class. Her interest in children and the law continued, and she decided to stay at Yale an extra year to continue work at the Yale Child Study Center. At the center, she studied child development, extending her expertise in children's legal rights in the context of how children develop emotionally and intellectually. She worked in the nursery, analyzed language development, assisted with diagnostic tests, and studied children's literature. She also collaborated on a book, *Beyond the Best Interests of the Child*, which proposed methods the courts could use to insure that custody decisions were in the child's best interest.

As graduation approached for the couple, the question of whether to continue their romance remained unresolved. Bill never wavered from his determination to return to Arkansas, and Hillary still felt she needed to pursue a law career in one of the larger cities. It was an agonizing period for both young people.

In the spring of 1973, Bill left for Arkansas. Hillary decided to move to Cambridge, Massachusetts, to work with Marion Wright Edelman in her new organization, the Children's Defense Fund. Different career plans had apparently ended the young couple's romance.

YOUNG LAWYER

Hillary had wanted to work for the Children's Defense Fund since first meeting Marion Wright Edelman three years before. Ms. Edelman had begun her career as an attorney for the NAACP, the pioneer civil rights organization. She had founded the Children's Defense Fund "to create a viable, long-range institution to bring about reforms for children."

One of the organization's primary goals is to fully implement the Head Start program. Head Start provides poor pre-school children the medicine, nutrition, and guidance necessary to succeed in school. Although the program, founded in the late 1960s, has generally been considered a success, even by most critics of social programs, it has never been fully funded by the federal government. For example, in 1988 only 16% of eligible children participated in the program.

From its beginning, the Children's Defense Fund has been controversial. Some critics view it as a pressure group advocating wasteful government spending; others are wary of any group which argues for a larger federal role in children's lives. They fear that the right of parents to raise their children as they think best is put at risk when the government becomes too deeply involved in a family's decisions. The controversy over the role of government in the education and protection of children has been a part of the American political debate since the public school movement of the early nineteenth century, and has continued through the debates over child labor laws of the early twentieth century, to the present day.

At the Children's Defense Fund, Hillary worked as a staff attorney, responsible for researching ways to change laws protecting children. However, Hillary was not to stay long at the Children's Defense Fund.

1973 was another critical year in U.S. history. The last U.S. soldiers came home from Vietnam. The Supreme Court handed down the *Roe v. Wade* decision, which precluded states from passing laws outlawing abortion. And the Watergate scandal threatened the presidency of Richard Nixon. "Watergate" involved a series of crimes which President Nixon's 1972 campaign workers committed in their efforts to insure his reelection. The most famous incident was a break-in at the Democratic Party's National Headquarters in a Washington D.C., office building called The Watergate. As 1974 approached, the country's attention was riveted on a Congressional investigation of the scandal.

In January of that year, Hillary received a call from John Doar, a lawyer working with the House Judiciary Committee, which was investigating President Nixon's possible role in hiding his campaign's involvement in Watergate. Doar asked Hillary to come to work on his staff. Although Hillary loved her work with the Children's Defense Fund, an offer from Washington to work with the Committee was too good to turn down.

Hillary's work there involved researching legal procedures. She spent long hours reading law books, and writing guidelines for the Committee to follow. But as it became evident that President Nixon was involved in the scandal, Hillary realized she was a participant in an historical series of events.

As the Watergate investigation developed, a series of recorded conversations between President Nixon and his top aides became the central issue. Nixon had earlier installed a recording system in his office. The House Judiciary Committee demanded to hear certain tapes on which they believed the

Watergate break-in was discussed by the president and his aides. When Nixon refused to turn over the tapes, the Judiciary Committee took its plea to the Supreme Court, where finally the White House was ordered to release the tapes.

One of Hillary's assignments was to listen to the White House tapes. She spent many hours locked in a small office, with an armed guard outside the door, listening to and transcribing the conversations between President Nixon and his aides as they discussed ways to keep the American people from discovering the truth about the Watergate break-in. The tapes eventually provided the evidence that forced Richard Nixon to resign his office, and Hillary was one of the first Americans to hear them.

Working on the Committee was difficult for Hillary. She worked seven-day weeks, often not leaving her office until midnight. But Hillary remembers it as an exhilarating time. "It was a real positive experience because the system worked. It was done in a very professional, careful way. . . Never have I been prouder to be a lawyer and to be an American than I was during those months."

Her experience with the House Judiciary Committee also deepened her interest in politics. Children's issues were still a primary concern, but the process of watching government up close during this dramatic period strengthened her conviction her that young, idealistic people should become involved in public affairs.

President Nixon resigned on August 8, 1974. It was a bittersweet day for Hillary. Though she was convinced that Nixon should no longer be chief executive, she knew the forced resignation of a president, especially so soon after the end of the Vietnam War, would further demoralize the nation.

While in Washington, Hillary shared a house with Sarah Ehrman, an old friend from the McGovern campaign. She also met several influential people who were impressed by the young lawyer; she took time out from her busy schedule for job interviews with some prestigious Washington law firms. Almost without exception the interviewers were impressed, and wanted her to join their firms. Hillary had other choices; she could establish herself as a prominent Washington attorney, or return to the Children's Defense Fund.

But there was still the matter of Bill Clinton, now teaching at the University of Arkansas Law School, and preparing to run for Congress from the Third Congressional District. They had stayed in touch by phone and through letters; now Hillary decided to pay him a visit. She traveled to Fayetteville, where the University of Arkansas is located. She thought the town was lovely. Bill introduced her to Wylie Davis, Dean of the Law School. He was so impressed by Hillary that he immediately asked her to apply for a job teaching at the Law School. She thanked him for the offer, but said she was still undecided about the next step in her career.

Hillary returned to Washington, and considered the job offers from the Washington law firms. She knew such employment would involve years of hard work, but the financial rewards, and her ability to impact the issues she cared about, would be great. But she could not get Arkansas, and Bill, out of her mind. After a few days of consideration, she called Dean Davis and told him she would take the teaching job.

She asked her friend Sarah Ehrman to drive her to Arkansas. Sarah agreed, but only because it would give her time to talk Hillary out of the move, which many of her friends thought a disastorous decision. During the two-day drive to Fayetteville, Sarah asked her repeatedly: "Are you sure you want to move to Arkansas?" She could not believe Hillary would give up her many opportunities in Washington to move to a small rural state to teach in a state university. She was determined to talk Hillary into returning to Washington.

For two days Sarah persisted. Hillary listened without comment. As they drove into Fayetteville, Sarah intensified her pleading. "For God's sake, Hillary, are you crazy? Why are you doing this?" she asked again.

Hillary smiled at Sarah and said, simply, "I love him." Sarah realized then there was nothing she could say to sway Hillary.

Hillary arrived in Fayetteville in August, and quickly began preparing for her first year as a law professor. She was assigned to teach criminal law, civil procedure, and children's law. But she also explored her new home, and soon decided that she was going to be happy in the small town atmosphere. "I liked people tapping me on the shoulder at the grocery store and saying 'Aren't you that lady professor at the law school?'" she recalls. In some ways, Fayetteville reminded her of Park Ridge. The people were friendly and helpful, and had many of the same values.

When Hillary arrived, Bill was in the middle of his first political campaign. He was running against John Paul Hammerschmidt, a popular Republican incumbent. Few people expected him to win, but he was gaining attention as an intelligent, attractive young candidate.

The campaign needed Hillary's help. Bill was charismatic, dedicated, and hard-working—but his campaign style was haphazard. He would return to his Fayetteville home, after a day of meeting voters, with the names of important contacts falling from his pockets. His volunteer campaign workers complained about the chaos. With her usual energy and efficiency, Hillary began organizing his campaign. She assigned people specific tasks, arranged Bill's schedule, and helped to write and edit his speeches. Bill was grateful for her help, and told reporters that Hillary was "far better organized, more in control, more intelligent and more eloquent than I am."

Hillary even invited her family down to help with Bill's campaign. Although the Rodhams still had doubts about Hillary moving permanently to Arkansas, they supported her decision. Even Hugh Sr., a life-long Republican, agreed to interrupt his retirement to come to Arkansas and help.

Bill's campaign quickly improved, and some observers began to say he might win. But the incumbent was too well entrenched. Bill lost the race, but did receive a higher percentage of votes, 48.2, than any previous challenger. Political observers would keep their eye on young Bill Clinton.

After the campaign, Hillary's mother and father

returned to Park Ridge. But her brothers enjoyed Fayetteville, and decided to stay and take classes at the university.

During the campaign, Hillary had traveled the 24 counties that comprised the Third District, and she was impressed by the state's beauty. She also liked the fact that everyone seemed to know each other, and loved the warm, southern graciousness, and deep concern for family she found in the small towns. And her experiences at the law school were positive. In a short time, Hillary felt at home in Arkansas. "I loved the university. I loved the law school. I loved my colleagues. I made some of the best friends I ever had in my life. It was just a wonderful experience for me."

One day Hillary was concerned about a student who had not been in class. When she called information and requested the student's number, the operator, instead of looking up the number, simply told her the student was not at home. The young man had gone camping, the operator said. Hillary hung up the phone, shaking her head. The operator knew the person she was trying to contact. This was a long way from impersonal, anonymous Washington, D. C..

After the campaign, Hillary and Bill enjoyed

working as colleagues on the law school faculty. Bill was known as an easy going teacher. Hillary, however, was considered a hard taskmaster who demanded the most from her students. One student remembers that "she was highly intellectual, aggressive, blunt, very articulate, and fairly tough." Some students were initially intimidated. "Some of the male students were not used to being taught by a woman with that kind of intellect," the student continues. "I think it took some of them a little while to get used to it. But as time went on, people warmed up to that and got comfortable."

Dean Davis was convinced he had made the right decision by offering Hillary a job. "She was really great. She was great in criminal law—she was great in everything she did."

Much as they had at Yale, Hillary and Bill quickly gathered a large group of friends. They had dinner parties, went to football games, and played volleyball and card games. One thing Hillary discovered about Bill was his competitive nature. He loved to win at everything he did.

It became increasingly clear to their friends that Hillary and Bill were very much in love. One of Bill's friends remembers "Bill wanted her to like Arkansas. He was crazy about her, and he wanted to marry her."

As much as she liked Arkansas, Hillary still wondered if she had made a mistake by leaving Washington. After her first year of teaching, she decided to take a trip north to visit old friends. Bill stayed behind in Fayetteville.

When Hillary returned from her trip, Bill picked her up at the airport. Hillary, who thought they were heading to her apartment, noticed they were taking a different route. When she asked Bill where they were going, Bill gave her a strange answer: "I bought that house you like," he said.

Hillary asked him what house he was talking about. Bill reminded her that shortly before her trip she had noticed a small house for sale and had remarked that it was pretty.

Hillary said she had never been inside it.

"Well, I bought it," Bill said. "So I guess we'll have to get married now."

When she recovered from her surprise, Hillary accepted the proposal. They set a wedding date for October 11, 1975, only two months away. Bill spent much of his time, outside the classroom, painting the small house, while Hillary made arrangments for the wedding. The affair was a small, private ceremony. Invited guests included family and friends from Yale and the law school faculty. Roger Clinton

Jr., Bill's half-brother, acted as best man. Hillary chose to keep her maiden name of Rodham, and Bill supported her in this decision. After the wedding reception, Bill and Hillary, along with the entire Rodham family, left for a honeymoon in Acapulco.

Hillary Rodham had decided to abandon a successful career as a Washington lawyer and move to Arkansas in order to marry the man she loved. But it was a decision that infuriated some of her friends. They thought she was making the same mistake Hillary had warned others against back at Main East High School—relinquishing a cherished goal for a man. Hillary did not attempt to rebut their criticisms. She had done what she thought was right. "It's so easy to find yourself editing feelings and beliefs based on what people may think," she said later. "You only have one life to live. I knew my relationship with Bill was very important to me." For Hillary Rodham there was no looking back. She had joined her future with Bill Clinton's, for better or for worse.

VICTORY AND DEFEAT

After their honeymoon, Hillary and Bill returned to teaching at the law school. But they both hoped they would not stay in Fayetteville much longer. Bill had plans on moving to Little Rock, the state capital, as an elected official.

Bill had had a conversation with Jim Guy Tucker, the Arkansas Attorney General. Tucker told him that he was going to run for Congress, and that Bill should try for the soon-to-be-vacant office of Attorney General. Bill was intrigued by the idea, and began planning a campaign.

In the meantime, Hillary continued to teach classes, and to promote community issues of special interest to her. She formed a group committed to reforming the laws covering rape and sexual assault. She also helped start a rape crisis center for victim counseling, and won funding from lawyer groups in Arkansas for a legal aid center to provide representation for poor people.

One story from this time reveals Hillary's growing resourcefulness as a lawyer. One day she received a call and was told that a woman who preached on the streets of Fayetteville had been arrested for disturbing the peace. A judge had decided to send the woman to a state mental institution for observation. Hillary thought the judge was wrong, and went to the jail to talk to the woman.

The street preacher convinced Hillary she was not crazy. "I just love the Lord," the woman said. But she steadfastly refused to stop her street preaching. Hillary continued to talk to her, and discovered the woman had family in California. "People need the Lord in California, too," Hillary told her. She knew the woman could not remain free in Arkansas, and so suggested to the judge that it would be cheaper to buy a ticket to California than to put the woman into an institution. The judge agreed, and the preacher left for California to continue her religious work.

During these years, Hillary also wrote a series of articles for scholarly journals, such as the *Harvard Educational Review.* The articles advocated a wider range of legal rights for children, and argued that in special situations children should have the same constitutional rights as adults. The underlying legal philosophy in the writings is that a child under a specified age, usually eighteen in the United States, should not automatically be considered property of the family, a legal precedent extending back to the eighteenth century. Hillary wrote that children should be evaluated as individuals by the court. If the child is determined to be "competent," a legal term indicating that an person is capable of speaking for him or herself in a law court, he or she should enjoy the full rights of citizenship.

There is an active counter-argument to Hillary's proposals in the field of children's law, supported by scholars who say that allowing the courts to determine if a child is competent, would create more problems than it solves. They fear that any weakening of parental authority would make parents less involved in their children's lives, because the child would no longer take parental guidance as seriously. They also say that liberating children from parental authority would end compulsory schooling, because children could no longer be legally required to stay in school.

In her writings, Hillary entered a lively debate about the rights of children in modern society. The articles were written for a relatively small group of intellectuals who study the changing roles of children and families. She probably never thought her work would later be forced into the center of her husband's political career. At the time, she was a young professor, actively pursuing a career in her field of expertise.

Hillary has said many times that she loved teaching and living in Fayetteville. "We had a wonderful life there. The pace of life was so much slower. I miss that in our lives now." But this happy period was coming to a close. In 1976, Bill won election as the Arkansas Attorney General. The win meant a move to Little Rock, the state capital. In Arkansas, the Attorney General, who serves as the state's attorney in court cases and also controls the state police, is the second most powerful state leader. Although they were sad to leave the little house in Fayetteville and their friends at the university, both Hillary and Bill were excited about Bill's first political office.

After Bill was sworn in as Attorney General, Hillary began looking for a new job. The Rose Law Firm, the oldest law firm west of the Mississippi River, offered her the chance to become one of the first women in the state hired by a major firm. But her gender was not the only reason the Rose Law Firm wanted Hillary on their staff. As one Little Rock attorney said, "Putting the issue of gender aside, she ranks among the top of Arkansas' trial lawyers. She just hasn't backed away from a fight."

However, the new job did put pressure on Hillary. Many male clients of the firm were uncomfortable around her. Not only was she a woman, but also a Northerner with a sharply analytical mind, and sometimes a brusque manner.

Although she performed varied legal tasks, Hillary continued taking on children's cases, often without pay. Usually these cases involved conflicts surrounding divorce. Hillary always argued for the best interests of the child.

In 1977, she received a high honor when President Jimmy Carter appointed her to the national board of directors of the Legal Services Corporation, a federally funded agency that helps poor people in civil cases, such as disputes with landlords. The job involved frequent travel to Washington.

She also started an organization called the Arkansas Advocates for Children and Families. The group studied the problems facing poor children in the state, and pressured politicians to fund programs to help them. Hillary served as the group's first president.

Bill's tenure as Attorney General was successful. He pushed for stronger ethics laws for politicians, and argued that utility companies charged unfair rate increases to Arkansas citizens. He also worked with the state police to bring down the crime rate. Bill was undoubtedly the rising star of Arkansas politics.

It was a busy time for the young couple. But, as usual, they found time to make new friends and to stay in touch with old ones. In Little Rock, they bought another small house, where they entertained often. As in law school, conversation at the dinner parties was usually about politics and public policy. But occasionally, Bill played his saxophone for friends, or they listened to records and danced.

Friends were impressed that Bill shared in the household duties. There was no question in the Clinton-Rodham house that necessary chores were a joint responsibility.

As the election year of 1978 approached, Bill decided to run for governor of Arkansas. Although only thirty-two, it was the natural next step for the ambitious Attorney General.

However, Hillary and Bill knew a gubernatorial campaign would put them both under intense media scrutiny. In the conservative southern state of

Arkansas, a wife with her own career, one who had kept her maiden name after marriage, could certainly be a political detriment. When Bill announced he would run for governor, a reporter asked him if he thought Hillary's name would become an issue. Bill said, "I hope not." But both he and Hillary knew it would.

During the campaign, Hillary was criticized for keeping her maiden name, for having a career outside the home, and for the articles she had written on children's rights. Bill's opponents, in both the Democratic and Republican parties, also hoped that making an issue of Hillary's independence would make Bill appear weak. "If he could not control his wife, how could he control the state?" was their argument.

Bill and Hillary ignored their critics. In his speeches, Bill emphasized improving education and strengthening the state's economy. Hillary continued to perform her role as chief advisor. Bill won the election, capturing over 60% of the vote. When he assumed office in January of 1979, he became the youngest governor in the United States.

However, Bill's first term would be a difficult period for the couple. Hillary continued to be criticized by the media. The gown she wore to the inaugural ball was described as resembling "something like a modified leg-o'-mutton" by a newspaper columnist.

At that time, the governor of Arkansas served a short, two-year term. Bill would attempt to solve several severe state problems in the first term. He pushed the state legislature to increase spending on education, and to merge school districts to create more balanced funding; to reform the method used to increase utility rates; and to raise car licensing fees and use the money to repair the decaying road system.

It was a large agenda, and many Arkansans opposed it. They sought ways to undercut Bill's public support. One tactic was to portray Hillary as a radical feminist and outsider. She was criticized for her dress, for her hair, for working as a lawyer instead of as a homemaker. But the keeping of her maiden name after marriage brought on the heaviest attacks. Letters asking, "Don't you love your husband?" and accusing her of being "uppity" were delivered almost daily to the Governor's Mansion.

Hillary did not always help herself. One photograph, published throughout the state, showed the couple at a University of Arkansas football game. While the crowd, including football fan Bill Clinton, cheered and waved their arms, Hillary sat quietly reading a book. Hillary seemed to resent the public relations role the first lady was expected to play, and this attitude angered some Arkansans.

Shortly into his first term, Bill's popularity began to fade. When car license tag fees were increased, constituents protested. Although the money was to be used to fix roads, the increase angered many automobile owners. Bill had other troubles. His proposal to spend the money on the Arkansas education system was unpopular with many legislators, and teachers resisted taking a competency test.

But nothing hurt Bill's popularity more than President Carter's decision to house thousands of Cuban refugees, released by dictator Fidel Castro in 1980, at Fort Chaffee, Arkansas. The decision was unpopular, and when some detainees escaped in May, 1980, state residents were outraged. Then, in June, Fort Chaffee erupted into a riot, and fear spread throughout the state. Bill called out the National Guard and the rioters were stopped, but he was blamed for the violence.

Although 1980 was difficult for Bill's career, one happy event did occur on February 27, when Hillary gave birth to a daughter. The couple had attended natural childbirth classes, but the baby was positioned wrongly in the womb and had to be delivered by Caesarean section. After the delivery, Bill walked the hospital corridors cradling his new daughter in his arms. The couple named their new daughter Chelsea, after "Chelsea Morning," one of their favorite Judy Collins songs.

As the 1980 campaign began, it was clear that Bill was in political trouble. President Carter, also a Democrat, was running for reelection, and many Arkansans were still angry with the president for housing the Cubans at Fort Chaffee. Bill's reelection chances suffered as a consequence. His opponent in the campaign, businessman Frank White, ran a series of television commercials linking Bill to the unpopular Carter.

Bill's reelection effort also suffered because Hillary was busy with her job and the new baby, which left her little time to help with campaign strategy.

Frank White won the 1980 gubernatorial race by a slim margin, and Bill became the youngest ex-governor in the United States. It looked as though Bill's bright political star had fallen from the sky. However, Hillary's own career was soaring; she was named a full partner at the Rose Law Firm.

As the couple packed to move out of the

Governor's Mansion, they faced an uncertain future. While Bill's career had come to a halt, Hillary's career was progressing rapidly. Many of their friends worried about the strain on their marriage; clearly the new decade was going to be a stressful time.

MS. CLINTON

When they were first married, Hillary and Bill faced a big decision. Bill had attended a Baptist church his entire life; Hillary was a Methodist. Should one of them change denominations, or should they worship separately? After discussing the matter, they agreed that their respective beliefs were too strong to change, and they decided to attend different churches.

Certainly Bill's faith was being sorely tested now. After leaving the Governor's Mansion, he became extremely depressed. Losing the election was of course a tough blow, but friends remember him as being more dejected than they had ever seen him. At this critical time, Bill's pastor at the Immanuel Baptist Church in Little Rock asked the Clintons to come along on a church-sponsored trip to Israel and the Holy Land. During the tour, they visited many sites mentioned in the Bible. Bill seemed to gain a new strength from the trip, and Hillary was delighted to see his old fighting spirit return.

Back in Arkansas, Bill had to decide about his future plans. Hillary suggested that he take a job in a law firm, and he thought the idea a good one. But they both hoped his career as a lawyer would only be temporary; he now planned to regain the governor's office in 1982.

After accepting a position with the law firm of Wright, Lindsey, and Jennings, a Rose Law Firm competitor, Bill traveled the state in his free time, making public appearances and delivering speeches. He apologized for the errors he made during his first term and promised to do a better job if the voters reelected him to office.

Hillary returned full-time to her busy law practice. After she was made a full partner in the firm, her work load increased. In addition to working on her own cases, she shared responsibility for managerial decisions. The increased responsibility did have one benefit, however. Soon she was earning nearly $400,000 a year, considerably more than the $35,000 Bill had earned as governor. In fact, during their entire married life, Hillary has consistently earned a larger salary than Bill.

During these trying years, when her husband was

often traveling and her career demanded greater amounts of time, Hillary also had to learn the complicated skills of motherhood. She was determined to give Chelsea a happy home, and the type of secure childhood she herself had enjoyed.

But, as most parents quickly discover, dealing with a new baby is sometimes difficult, especially on nights when the child cannot sleep. It was during the early morning hours of such a night when Hillary made her "breakthrough" as a mother. "It was one of those nights where you rocked her, you walked her, and you sang to her—you did everything, and she just kept crying," Hillary recalled later. "I remember saying to her, 'You know, Chelsea, you've never been a baby before and I've never been a mother before. We are just going to have to get through this together.' And that's kind of how I have lived it."

***

As the election year of 1982 approached, Hillary needed to make several decisions. She wanted Bill to regain the governorship, but many voters had shown they felt threatened by her. Although she shared many of the core values of Arkansans, such as a strong faith, and devotion to children and family, Bill's political opponents had succeeded in characterizing her as an enemy of those beliefs. She needed to correct this misconception.

Her appearance was part of the problem. The frumpy clothes and frizzy hair had left her open to criticism as a first lady who did not create a proper image, and they had a certain "hippy" aspect, which some Arkansans did not approve of. She replaced the big glasses with contact lenses; had her hair cut and styled; replaced the baggy dresses with smartly tailored suits; and, on occasion, wore lipstick and eye shadow, as another bow to fashion.

However, the most damaging criticism had been over her last name. When Chelsea was born, and a newspaper announced "Governor Bill Clinton and Hillary Rodham have a daughter," many readers were disturbed. One editorial said the announcement gave the impression that the couple was not married.

She finally decided to campaign as Hillary Clinton. "It [her maiden name] meant more to the constituents than it did to me," she said, and added that the controversy over her name had "interfered with people's perceptions of the kind of job Bill did."

Hillary was quick to point out that Bill had not

pressured her to make the change. "I joked one time that probably the only man in Arkansas who didn't ask me to change my name was my husband." Bill agreed with her that what she called herself was purely her personal decision.

After she made the changes, Hillary received a great deal of positive press. Many of the same writers and reporters who had previously criticized her, now spoke of her in kinder terms. "The name change indicates that she's working at softening her image a bit," one former critic wrote.

But, many of her friends were unhappy. Betsey Wright, the Democratic Party activist Hillary and Bill had met in 1972, said, "I teared up. I had a lump in my throat." Another friend said it made her sad because she knew Hillary "wanted so badly not to lose her independence."

However, Hillary had made her decision, and despite any personal sadness she may have felt, she campaigned for Bill in her characteristically determined way. She was convinced her husband was good for Arkansas, and she worked hard to return him to office.

During the campaign, commentators began talking of Hillary as a more able politician than Bill. She was seen as the more articulate of the two, and

Hillary in her inaugural gown at the beginning of Bill's third term as Governor, in January 1985. (AP/Wide World Photos)

Dressed in their formal best, Hillary and Bill arrive at the White House to attend a dinner hosted by President Ronald Reagan, in February, 1986. (AP/Wide World Photos)

quicker to reach decisions. Hillary was suddenly being discussed as a political figure in her own right.

She had a generally positive effect on the campaign. Her changes in name and appearance won support, and she continued to make many strategic campaign decisions. She may have softened her image, but within the campaign she was still the same Hillary, and that meant she could be more exacting than her husband. One 1982 campaign worker remembers: "She had the toughness to complement Bill Clinton. He doesn't like to tell anybody no, and she knows how to do that."

Arkansans responded positively to the return of Bill and Hillary. Traveling around the state, Bill and Hillary realized many of the people who had voted against him in 1980 had merely wanted to "send him a message" about certain issues, but did not really want to replace him as governor. Now they were willing to give him a second chance at running the state.

Bill's chances were also helped by Frank White's failure to improve the lives of most Arkansans. White campaigned for reelection by using the same strategy that had worked in 1980, depicting Bill and Hillary as radicals out of touch with the average voter. Bill's speeches, however, stressed the need to improve education, and to attract higher paying jobs to the state.

Bill won the 1982 election with 54.7% of the vote. His political career was still alive. As the young family returned their belongings to the small living quarters within the Governor's Mansion, Bill knew he owed much of his comeback to the efforts, and personal sacrifices, of Hillary. They were forging the bonds of a political marriage unlike any seen before in American politics.

ARKANSAS DECADE

When he returned to office, Bill's first priority was to improve the state's education system. The schools in Arkansas ranked near the bottom in every national education survey, and he knew it was time for improvement.

To accomplish his education goals, Bill needed the legislature to pass a number of reforms. He also knew improvements in education would cost money, and that meant raising taxes. Although Arkansas had the lowest tax rates in the country, raising taxes in the state was difficult—even the suggestion had destroyed several politicians' careers. The people of the state would have to be convinced the measure was absolutely necessary.

Bill decided the best way to make the public aware of what needed to be done was to form a public committee to travel the state and to gather information from local school boards, teachers, and concerned parents. The committee would then formalize the reform recommendations and he would ask the legislature to put them into law. The people selected to sit on the committee would be critical to its success, and Bill labored over the selection process.

But one committee selection was easy. Bill named Hillary to chair the group, though it was politically risky to appoint his wife to such an important post. Announcing Hillary's selection, he said she would "guarantee that I will have a person who is closer to me than anyone else, overseeing a project that is more important than anything else. I don't know if it's a politically wise move, but it's the right thing to do."

Hillary was enthusiastic about the new challenge. The public education she had received in Park Ridge public schools had prepared her for a successful life, and she wanted the children of Arkansas to have the same opportunity. "We have today an historic obligation to equalize funding and to improve education," she announced, and began traveling the state to solicit suggestions and to gain support for the initiatives.

Hillary's task was helped when, in 1983, the National Commission on Excellence in Education issued a report on the quality of the country's schools. The report, entitled "A Nation At Risk," spoke of a "rising tide of mediocrity" in education, and said that inadequate education was the gravest threat to the country's future success. Suddenly the nation's attention was focused on improving schools, and education reform became one of the hottest political topics in the country. Bill and Hillary found themselves on the leading edge of a national debate.

During her travels around the state, Hillary made certain that the ideas and opinions of local leaders were heard. Often she would begin a meeting with a roomful of people who were opposed to any education reforms that would necessitate higher taxes. But after she had made the case that economic growth would not come to the state until the work force was better educated, most would leave the meeting convinced it was time to sacrifice for their children's future. The committee was soon known as the "Hillary Committee."

When the group's work was finished, it issued a list of recommendations, including mandatory kindergarten, smaller class sizes, longer school years, better school counselors, teacher competency tests, and more class credits required for high school graduation. Most concerned parents supported the recommendations, but one suggestion created a political firestorm.

The controversy erupted over the so-called "teacher testing" part of the bill. This section required teachers to pass a competency test before they could receive a pay raise. The teachers protested; hundreds announced they would not take the test. The Arkansas Education Association spoke out against the move, and when Bill made it clear that teachers would have to take the test before he asked the legislature to raise taxes, the attacks on Bill and Hillary intensified. One school librarian was quoted as saying the Clintons were "lower than snakes."

Teachers booed Hillary's speeches, and catcalls often met her when she toured a school. Although disappointed in the reaction, she continued her work, refusing to let criticism sway her from what she thought was the right path for the state's students.

The controversy over the teacher competency test brought Bill, and indirectly Hillary, national attention. Newspapers with national circulation like *The New York Times* and *The Washington Post*, carried articles about the dispute. Bill was a guest on the CBS Sunday morning news show, *Face The Nation*, where he presented his case for the teacher competency tests.

Eventually, the vast majority of teachers took the test. When the results were announced, Bill asked the legislature to implement the additional improvements, including higher teacher salaries. Hillary lobbied the legislature to pass the education reform bill. During one of her presentations to a room of legislators who were opposed to the reforms, Hillary was so persuasive that one politician stood up and said, "It looks like we've elected the wrong Clinton."

Finally, in 1985, most of the reforms became law. But the fight for better schools continued. Reforming the long-neglected system would take years. In her work in education, Hillary had become convinced that a child's pre-school years are the most critical; studies indicated that if children from disadvantaged homes received help in their first years of life their chances of succeeding in school were greatly improved. Hillary focused her attention on pre-school children.

Hillary believed the best way to help disadvantaged pre-schoolers was to work with the parents one-on-one, in effect teaching them how to become their child's first teacher. After considering several methods to accomplish this goal, she selected a program called the Home Instruction Program for Preschool Youngsters, or HIPPY.

From the beginning HIPPY was a success. Trained teachers visited homes and taught parents how to help their children prepare for school. When the program was fully enacted, the children who participated succeeded in school at much higher levels than children who had no pre-school instruction. The HIPPY program still continues in Arkansas, and is one of the successes of Bill's twelve years as governor.

As the decade continued, Hillary developed a national reputation as an advocate for children. She helped create a national program, financed by the Rockefeller Foundation, to help troubled older children succeed at school; and was appointed to the William T. Grant Foundation's Commission on Work, Family and Citizenship. Her work and writings on family and education issues were studied by lawyers and educators in other states.

During these years, while busy with her unpaid work with education reform, Hillary continued her duties at the Rose Law Firm, where she was particularly noted for her sharp, analytical mind, and the ability to focus on the central issue in most legal disagreements. She worked long hours, often staying in the office until midnight. She specialized in "intellectual property" disputes, involving conflicts over the ownership of patents and copyrights.

During the 1980s, Hillary also served as a paid director on corporate boards, including the TCBY yogurt company and the Wal-Mart discount store chain. Wal-Mart is headquartered in Bentonville, Arkansas, and Hillary was the first woman on its board of directors. During her tenure with Wal-Mart, she helped liberalize the company's policies on the hiring and promotion of women and minorities. When the rapidly growing company, founded by the late Sam Walton, was criticized for its environmental record, she helped formalize an environmental protection strategy.

Another company Hillary joined in the 1980s was Tyson Foods, one of the nation's largest poultry producers. Tyson Foods is one of Arkansas' largest employers, and the legislature, occasionally at Bill's urging, has granted the company exemptions from state laws. When it became clear that Tyson Foods was responsible for some of the pollution in Arkansas' rivers and streams, Hillary's position on the Board of Directors raised questions about the close relationship between the governor's wife and the company. Although no one charged that any laws were broken, Hillary's paid position with the company seemed inappropriate to some.

Hillary's life in Arkansas was full and exciting. Chelsea started school, and even with her busy schedule, Hillary tried to spend time with her daughter every day. Hillary or Bill drove Chelsea to school in the morning. When out of town, Hillary made video tapes of herself and left them for her daughter to watch.

Chelsea, an excellent student, skipped a grade in school. She enjoys sports, and played on softball and soccer teams. She also loves ballet, and has danced in recitals from an early age. In Little Rock, her parents tried to attend every game, where Bill would sometimes embarrass her by cheering loudly. On weekends and holidays, it was not uncommon to see the family playing softball or touch football on the mansion's lawn.

Another characteristic of the Clintons is their informality. One old friend recalls calling at the mansion late at night. Hillary and Bill greeted him and his wife in their bathrobes, and immediately invited them inside to have a late snack in the kitchen.

Much of the family's entertaining took place around the kitchen table. Friends would gather to snack on treats from the refrigerator and play cards or tell stories. Both Clintons are skilled storytellers. Hillary was especially good at retelling episodes from her law practice, including anecdotes about some of the colorful characters from the more rural areas of Arkansas. She often illustrated her stories by pretending to spit tobacco juice from the side of her mouth. Bill, not to be outdone, mastered an authentic Arkansas hog call.

The 1980s was a decade of great political success for the Clintons. Although his opponents continued characterizing him as a liberal who was out of touch with the average Arkansan, the voters returned Bill to office in 1984, 1986, and 1990. He was always quick to give Hillary much of the credit for his success. There was even talk of Hillary succeeding her husband as governor, including reports that she had asked political supporters if they thought she could win. But Hillary publicly denied any interest in running for governor, and stated that she worked best in a supporting role.

By 1988, Bill had a national reputation as a bright, progressive governor, and many pundits thought Bill would run that year for the Democratic

Party's nomination for President of the United States. Bill had never denied that he was interested in being president some day. It had been a dream since he was a boy. But he was not convinced 1988 was the best year for him to run. Chelsea was only seven, and a national campaign would separate her from Hillary and Bill for long periods of time. Although he received promises of support from many Democrats, Bill finally decided not to attempt a campaign in 1988.

However, Bill continued working in national politics, and his reputation continued to grow. He served as Chairman of the National Governors Association, and as leader of a group of moderate Democrats called the Democratic Leadership Council. Hillary also traveled nationally, speaking and lecturing about her work in Arkansas, and promoting the Children's Defense Fund.

Life for the family in Arkansas was rich and rewarding. However, it was almost certain that Bill would eventually make a run for the presidency. When that time came, the family would be forced onto the national stage. As the fall presidential campaign between Vice-President George Bush and Massachusetts Governor Michael Dukakis approached, Hillary and Bill thought that they had at least four years before they would have to contend with the national media. But they were not counting on the publicity that would be generated by a speech Bill was scheduled to give at the 1988 Democratic National Convention.

CAMPAIGN ISSUE

Bill was flattered when Michael Dukakis asked him to put his name into nomination at the Democratic National Convention. Dukakis, who was not popular in the south, hoped Bill's nominating speech would win him southern support.

But the speech would almost end Bill's career — and it was Hillary who did the most to salvage it.

Bill usually writes his own speeches, but at the convention the Dukakis campaign staff insisted Bill read an address they had prepared. Bill's delivery stumbled at the more awkward passages of the poorly written speech. The crowd, impatient for the nominee to appear, were encouraged by the Dukakis campaign workers to call out "We want Mike!" at every pause. The speech, scheduled for 15 minutes, took 33 to deliver, and Bill had to stop several times to ask for quiet, and was applauded only when he said the words, "in conclusion."

The speech, captured on nationwide television, made Bill the laughingstock of the nation. *The Washington Post* story about the speech was entitled "The Numb and the Restless," and many journalists said Bill had destroyed his career. The most damaging comment came from the late night talk show host Johnny Carson, who called Bill "a windbag."

Hillary knew something had to be done quickly. Bill, shocked by the negative reaction, and facing a future as the brunt of comedian's jokes, was unsure how to respond. Hillary, however, jumped into action. She called her friends Harry Thomason and his wife Linda Bloodworth-Thomason, Arkansas natives who worked in Hollywood as the producers of *Designing Women* and *Evening Shade*, two highly successful network situation comedies. They devised a strategy. Because Johnny Carson was, at the time, the top late night talk show host, and had already made several jokes about the speech, Hillary and her two friends convinced Bill that he should appear on the show. The producers of *The Tonight Show* agreed for Bill to appear if he would play his saxophone with the band.

It was a risky maneuver, however. Johnny Carson's sharp wit was legendary, and if Bill's

As daughter Chelsea looks on, Hillary waves to the crowd after Bill's official entry into the 1992 presidential campaign on October 3, 1991. (AP/Wide World Photos)

appearance was not a success, the damage to his public image could be devastating. But Hillary finally convinced him it was the only way to salvage his reputation.

The night of Bill's appearance, Carson delivered a long and rambling introduction that included trivia about Arkansas and Bill's personal biography. It was a hilarious parody of Bill's speech at the Democratic Convention, and the audience roared with laughter. They clearly expected Johnny to have an easy time making jokes at the relatively unknown politician's expense.

But when Johnny finally finished his introduction, Bill entered the set laughing, and continued laughing at Johnny's pokes at him. He showed such good humor that Johnny seemed to enjoy his visit. Bill finished his visit by playing the saxophone with the band, and when he left the stage, Johnny praised him for his sense of humor, and admitted he would have to find a new target for his jokes.

The national media covered Bill's appearance with Carson; there was general agreement Bill had won over his critics with his ability to joke about himself. He had saved his political career; and Hillary was chiefly responsible for mapping out the successful strategy.

After the 1988 presidential campaign was over, and George Bush had overwhelmingly defeated Michael Dukakis, Hillary was appointed to a special committee, established by the American Bar Association, to investigate ways to end racially segregated schools. She also served as national chairperson of the Children's Defense Fund.

Also in 1988, the *National Law Journal*, the leading national publication for lawyers, named Hillary as one of the "100 Most Influential Lawyers In America." She was again named to the list in 1990. Clearly, Hillary had reached the top of the legal profession.

In 1990, Bill was selected as co-chair of a presidential summit on education held at the University of Virginia. The meeting of the nation's governors was a great success, and President Bush thanked him publicly for his help. Hillary attended the summit with Bill, and made a strong impression on President Bush when she pointed out to him that the United States was ranked seventeenth in the world in the rate of infant mortality (the number of babies that die before their first birthday).

The President responded, "Hillary, whatever are you talking about? Our health-care system is the envy of the world."

"Not if you want to keep your child alive to his first birthday," she replied.

Bush disagreed with her argument, but promised to check the statistics. The next day the President handed Bill a note that read: "Tell Hillary she was right." Hillary has always been willing to press the issues she cares deeply about to anyone she thinks can help. And this includes the President of the United States.

During his 1990 reelection campaign for governor, Bill faced stiff opposition in the Democratic primary. One opponent was Tom McRae, and in the middle of the primary campaign, when Bill was away from Arkansas, McRae held a news conference and charged Bill with neglecting the state's needs.

Much to McRae's surprise, Hillary was in the audience. Angry at what she perceived as groundless charges against Bill's record, made when he was not present to defend himself, she challenged McRae.

When the stunned McRae repeated his charge that Bill was more interested in his national political ambitions than in serving as Arkansas's governor, Hillary pulled out a report issued by the Winthrop Rockefeller Foundation, a public policy group, which praised Bill's efforts to improve the state.

After reading the report, she paused dramatically before reading the name of the chairman of the foundation when the report had been issued — Tom McRae. Then she pressed McRae to reveal why he was now criticizing Bill when he had previously praised him. McRae grew increasingly flustered, and left the stage as soon as possible.

Hillary's actions at this press conference became a hot topic of discussion around the state. While some newspaper columnists, and some political opponents, accused her of being "pushy," others admired her determination. One columnist wrote that Hillary "set out to eat McRae's lunch and didn't stop until she'd finished off his dessert."

Bill won reelection in 1990, but the campaign was filled with many of the same personal charges against Bill and Hillary that would reappear in the 1992 presidential campaign, including insinuations that Bill had had extra-marital sexual affairs. There were also claims that the Rose Law Firm benefited unethically from Hillary's position as Arkansas' first lady. Hillary thought the national Republican Party, afraid that Bill would run for president in 1992, wanted to destroy his reputation in the 1990 gubernatorial race. Chelsea was now old enough to understand, and to be hurt, by the politically motivated attacks on her parents, and Hillary had to explain to her daughter that politics is often unpleasant.

After winning reelection, Bill announced it would be his last term as governor. It was time to move on toward national office, or retire from politics and again take up the practice of law. Both United States senators from Arkansas were Democrats, and long-time friends of the Clintons. Bill could not challenge them by running for the Senate. His only alternative was to run for the presidency in 1992.

Hillary did not think it was realistic Bill could be elected president in 1992. In 1991, after the success of the Gulf War, when American troops forced Saddam Hussein's army out of Kuwait, President Bush's popularity in opinion polls rose to record levels. Most of the presumed Democratic candidates, including Senator Al Gore of Tennessee and Senator Bill Bradley of New Jersey, announced they would not run in 1992. They thought going up against President Bush in 1992 would be a waste of time, and decided to wait until 1996, when Bush would not be in the race.

Bill, however, thought President Bush was neglecting many of the serious problems facing the country. The economy was not growing, health care

Hillary with Bill during an important interview on the CBS "60 Minutes" program on January 26, 1992, when rumors of his extra-marital affairs had the candidate dropping in popularity polls. (AP/Wide World Photos)

The Clintons work together on a plane between campaign stops in March, 1992. (AP/Wide World Photos)

costs were rising, and education reform was stalled nationwide. Many of the same problems Bill and Hillary had faced in Arkansas also plagued the nation, and Bill thought the country needed a president who would focus on the country's domestic problems. He sensed many Americans shared his concern over the direction the country was taking. But to run for president was an awesome task. Both Hillary and Bill knew the campaign would be long and hard. Chelsea would be exposed to the same type of personal attacks experienced in the 1990 campaign, only this time the charges would be made on a national stage. As in 1988, the decision whether or not to run for president was difficult.

On October 3, 1991, Bill Clinton stood before the Old State House in Little Rock and announced his candidacy for the 1992 Democratic Party's nomination for president of the United States. "I don't want my child or your child to be part of a country that's coming apart instead of coming together," he said. It was a theme he would repeat over the next thirteen months, and a message that sustained him through one of the most hectic, and bitter, presidential campaigns in American history.

The other major candidates running for the Democratic nomination were former Governor Jerry Brown of California, Senators Bob Kerrey of Nebraska and Tom Harkin of Iowa, former Massachusetts Senator Paul Tsongas, and Virginia Governor Douglas Wilder. Bill quickly emerged as the front-runner, as commentators, and early primary voters, were impressed by his understanding of the issues, and his ability to make voters feel he was speaking directly to their concerns.

The New Hampshire primary was the first big race of the year. In many ways the state was perfect for Bill. Because the state is small, it allowed Bill to present himself personally to many of the voters, which is when he is probably most impressive. Most people who meet Bill Clinton come away impressed by his intelligence. But Paul Tsongas, from neighboring Massachusetts, had a definite "home field" advantage in New Hampshire.

Hillary campaigned as hard as Bill. She spoke to all types of groups, not limiting herself to the more traditional "women's groups" as had previous candidate's wives. Hillary was as impressive as her husband, and articles began appearing about the Bill-Hillary team.

Then the Clinton campaign pollsters saw trouble in their surveys. Many poll respondents expressed misgivings about Hillary's role in the campaign.

Although other politicians' wives have been crucial to their husband's success, a high percentage of the poll respondents felt Hillary's position as chief strategist was inappropriate. Others thought she neglected her family because of personal ambitions. In many ways, these were the same public perceptions that had troubled her in Arkansas. Campaign advisors suggested she take a less public profile while they determined the best way to deal with the voter's negative impression of her.

Hillary was depressed by the poll results. She was a devoted mother, and had committed a large portion of her career, usually without pay, toward improving children's lives. Recently, she had even traveled to France to research ways to more efficiently provide day care, health services, and education to needy children. And, most importantly, she had raised her daughter with love, and had fought to hold her family together when she and Bill suffered marital problems. Although she realized political perceptions often were grounded more in image than in fact, to be perceived as a woman who cared little for "family values" hurt her deeply. However, she accepted the pollsters' suggestion, and reduced her public appearances.

Then, before the Clinton campaign could work

out a strategy to deal with Hillary's image problem, the world caved in on Bill and Hillary—and she had no choice but to play a public role. In January of 1992, a supermarket tabloid ran an article alleging Bill had had a long-term affair with a woman in Arkansas named Gennifer Flowers. Ms. Flowers had previously denied similar rumors, but in the article she said she had been his mistress for ten years. When the national media picked up the story, Bill's campaign was severely damaged.

Some advisors in Bill's campaign suggested he drop out of the race. But Hillary, much as she had after the 1988 Democratic Convention fiasco, moved into action. She insisted they publicly attack the story, and when the popular CBS news show *60 Minutes* offered them the opportunity to appear together and discuss the allegations, they seized the opportunity.

The interview aired on January 26, after the Super Bowl. In response to the questions of Steve Kroft, the interviewer, Bill denied he had ever had an affair with Gennifer Flowers. While admitting he had made mistakes during his marriage, he refused to reveal any more of his personal life. But Hillary turned out to be the focus of the newscast. Her eyes often flashed with barely repressed anger as she refuted the story. When Kroft pressed for more details of their personal life, Hillary responded: "There isn't a person watching this who would feel comfortable sitting on this couch detailing everything that ever went on in their life and marriage." When Kroft continued questioning, she answered, "We've gone further than anybody we know of, and that's all we're going to say." Her performance was impressive, and stopped Bill's slide in the polls. Hillary's public display of devotion had helped save him from being driven from the race.

However, Hillary did make mistakes later in the primary season. In her hometown of Chicago, a reporter asked her about recent accusations made against her by Jerry Brown, who had criticized her work at the Rose Law Firm, and charged that Bill had "funneled" money to the firm. These were old charges, and Hillary denied them. Then she added that she was being criticized because of her successful career, and said: "I suppose I could have stayed home and baked cookies and had teas. But what I decided to do was pursue my profession, which I entered before my husband was in public life."

The so-called "cookie and teas" line became the next hotly debated story in a campaign that never lacked controversy. Media stories began appearing all over the country about the Clinton campaign's

Hillary speaks to a campaign rally during the final stretch of the long 1992 presidential campaign. (AP/Wide World Photos)

Hillary and Tipper Gore, wife of new Vice President Al Gore, wave to a joyous crowd during a victory celebration on November 4, 1992. (AP/Wide World Photos)

"Hillary Problem." Reporters interviewed women who did not work outside the home, and reported that many were hurt and insulted by the comment. Hillary apologized: "I can understand why some people thought that I was criticizing women who made different choices from the ones I had—in fact, criticizing the choice that my mother and a lot of dear friends have made. Nothing could be further from what I believe." But the controversy continued throughout the spring and into the summer.

In addition to the controversy over Hillary's comments, Bill had plenty of other worries, including charges that he had avoided the draft during the Vietnam War. However, he continued campaigning, and eventually won enough votes to win the Democratic nomination for president, although in the spring of 1992 most political pundits gave him little chance of winning in November. They were convinced he had been hurt beyond repair early in the primary campaign. The race seemed to be between President Bush and Ross Perot, a Texas billionaire who had entered the race and generated a great deal of grassroots support.

Polls indicated that Hillary's image was more of a problem than ever. She had to do something to change people's impressions of her. She chose a familiar stage to begin redefining her image—a commencement address at Wellesley. To the audience of young women, she said: "You may choose to be a corporate executive or a rocket scientist, you may run for public office, you may choose to stay home and raise your children—but you can now make any or all of those choices—and they can be the work of your life."

After making clear she supported women who worked at home, Hillary moved on to the issue that had concerned her since Yale Law School: "How we treat our children should be front and center of the agenda, or I believe it won't matter what else is on it. My plea is that you not only nurture the values that will determine the choices you make in your personal lives, but also insist on policies that include those values to nurture our nation's children."

In this speech, Hillary revealed her deepest concerns and beliefs. Women should have the opportunity to choose their own path in life, and should not be criticized for working inside the home any more than they should be criticized for pursuing public careers. And she let it be known that in both her public and private lives, her primary concern was for children. The speech received extensive national coverage, and began a re-evaluation of Hillary by many voters.

During June, some leaders in the Democratic Party suggested publicly that Bill was so damaged by the tough primary campaign that he should be denied the nomination. They wanted the National Convention, to be held in July in New York City, to select a different candidate.

When Bill selected Al Gore, a popular senator, as his vice-presidential running mate, his standing in the polls began to improve, although the attention of the media, and of President Bush, was focused on Ross Perot, who had stunned the nation by shooting to the top of most major polls. Then, during the Democratic Convention, Ross Perot surprised the country again by suddenly announcing he was dropping out of the race. Almost overnight, Bill's poll ratings moved up nearly thirty points. The Bush campaign, all its attention now focused on Bill, renewed its efforts to portray Hillary as an enemy of the family. Quotes from the articles on children's rights she had written in the 1970s were used to accuse her of comparing marriage to slavery, and of encouraging children to sue their parents to get out of doing chores. During the Republican Convention, in August of 1992, Pat Buchanan, a former presidential candidate, said Hillary was the enemy of everything traditional in American life.

Hillary, Bill, Al Gore, Tipper Gore, and their children acknowledge the cheers of the crowd on election night, November 3, 1992. (AP/Wide World Photos)

Hillary publicly shrugged off the attacks, saying "There's that kind of double bind women find themselves in. On the one hand, be smart, and stand up for yourself. On the other hand, don't offend anyone and don't step on toes, or you'll become somebody who no one likes because you are too assertive."

Hillary's long days of campaigning were made more pleasant when she met Tipper Gore, the wife of Al Gore. Tipper and Hillary became fast friends. However, Hillary did feel the need to return to Arkansas whenever possible to "make a cup of tea, hang out with Chelsea, take an afternoon nap. If I don't get back home, I don't feel grounded," she said. She tried to protect Chelsea from press attention by refusing requests for interviews with her daughter, and by guarding against unauthorized photographs in private moments.

As the campaign moved into its final weeks, Hillary's standing in the polls began to improve. Many voters were unhappy with the way the Republican Convention had focused so much attention on her, and wanted the campaign to be fought over economic issues.

Although Ross Perot re-entered the race in October, and participated in the three national debates,

Bill maintained his lead throughout the fall. On November 3, 1992, Bill Clinton was elected the 42nd President of the United States. And Hillary Rodham Clinton was going to be the First Lady, the most prominent and powerful woman in the nation.

FIRST LADY

Days after the election, media reports out of Little Rock, where the Clinton advisors were creating the new administration, began emphasizing Hillary's influence on the transition, and questioning if the American public would accept an activist first lady. One Republican advisor said Hillary would get "brushed back a bit." "People don't like the wife mucking about in the husband's affairs. She wasn't elected and they just don't like it," another said. It was suggested she would retreat to a more conventional first lady's role.

But Hillary and Bill had no plans to alter the combination that had served them so well over the years. She had always been his top advisor, and her impact was immediately apparent when Bill began announcing who would serve as members of his cabinet. Donna Shalala, who had worked with

Hillary at the Children's Defense Fund, was named Secretary of Health and Human Services, the department that administers Social Security and many other government social programs; Web Hubbel, appointed Assistant Attorney General, was a former partner in the Rose Law Firm; and Robert Reich, the new Secretary of Labor, was an old Yale friend of both Hillary and Bill.

Even before Bill was inaugurated, controversy surrounded the Clinton family. Chelsea is the first school age child to live in the White House since Amy Carter in the late 1970s. The Clintons have always been strong supporters of public schools, and Chelsea had attended city schools in Little Rock. But Hillary and Bill decided she should attend Sidwell Friends School, a private Quaker academy, when they moved to Washington. Their decision was determined by what they thought best for Chelsea, who faced a tough transition to a new environment. But the choice angered many, who thought Hillary and Bill were being hypocritical for removing Chelsea from public school.

The old problem of Hillary's dress continued to hound her when her choice of clothes for the inaguration was widely criticized by fashion designers and style critics. Her bright blue coat with a matching blue velour, wide-brimmed hat was labeled "unglamorous." One designer sniffed that she dressed in a "middle class" fashion. Another negative review called it "working woman chic."

However, clothes had never been Hillary's primary concern, and after Bill was sworn in she reverted to practical, professional dress. That her mind was on more important things became evident when it was announced she would have a large office in the West Wing of the White House, where the most important members of the president's staff have offices. Traditionally, the first lady's office has been in the East Wing. Hillary's West Wing office received a great amount of press. One national news magazine even printed a diagram of the White House, with arrows pointing out the office location.

Hillary would need the large office. Health care reform may be the most hotly debated issue of the entire Clinton Administration, and on January 25, the week after inauguration, Bill announced that Hillary would head the task force established to study the issue. Bill does not think the country can solve its economic problems, especially the federal budget deficit, until the rapid increase in health care costs are brought under control. On a more human level, it is estimated that 30 million Americans have no health insurance coverage. Announcing Hillary's appointment, Bill said she was "better at organizing and leading people from a complex beginning to a certain end than anybody I've ever worked with in my life." Hillary's top aide on the Health Care Task Force is another old friend, Ira Magaziner. Magaziner graduated from Brown University the same year Hillary graduated from Wellesley, also spoke at his commencement, and was featured in the same *Life* magazine article as Hillary. Later, Magaziner, also a Rhodes Scholar, met Bill at Oxford.

The task force's suggestions on health care will probably take the form of what is called "managed competition." The managed competition approach emphasizes the creation of large groups of people covered under one plan, in order to lower the premiums paid by the insured. It also calls for a national health care budget. Because America's health care costs have been rising much higher than the prices of other items, the advocates of this approach think it will be impossible to assure that all Americans have medical coverage until expenses are controlled. Creating a national health care budget, and holding costs within the specified limits, will be a difficult task, and Hillary's leadership skills will be put to a severe test.

Hillary is also concerned about the nation's welfare system. She believes that work is the best cure for poverty, and thinks our present system does not do enough to keep families together. She would prefer a welfare system that provides a way for people to work, and educate, themselves out of poverty. If her efforts on health care reform are successful, welfare reform will probably be the next problem she tackles.

One legal conflict that develops from Hillary's active participation in the government is created by the so-called "Bobby Kennedy" law. The law, passed after President Kennedy appointed his brother Attorney General, forbids a president from naming a family member to a paid government position. While Hillary does not receive a salary for her work, and does not specifically violate the law, critics charge that her appointment to the Health Care Task Force violates the law's intent. Others, including many of Bill and Hillary's critics, think the law is unconstitutional, and should never have been passed.

While the argument over the legality of Hillary's role continues, her powerful position could create problems inside the administration. As one political commentator says, "Who is going to tell the

The new First Couple walking down Pennsylvania Avenue during the presidential inaugural parade on January 20, 1993. (AP/Wide World Photos)

First Lady Hillary Rodham Clinton focuses on a speaker during a discussion on reforming the nation's health care system. (AP/Wide World Photos)

President that his wife is wrong?" There is a risk that Hillary's dual role of chief advisor, and presidential wife, could stifle the free flow of information and criticism which enables a president to make wise decisions. How Hillary and Bill handle this sensitive situation will help determine the degree of their success.

Another controversy has been over the Health Care Task Force's policy of closed meetings. Although the group has held some public meetings, much of the work has gone on behind closed doors. Again, there are two views of the legality, and wisdom, of holding secret meetings. Critics charge disclosure laws require the meetings to be open, and argue that the public should be aware of the group's operations. Supporters of the closed meeting policy point out that the Constitutional Convention of 1787 was held in secret, and insist that open meetings would allow the enemies of health care reform to sabotage the task force's work.

Every presidential administration has its own set of conflicts and disputes, and the Clinton Administration is certainly no exception. In the early months, several of the conflicts have developed out of Hillary's role in the new government. Clearly, Hillary is a new kind of first lady: the second most important person in the White House. But there have been other influential first ladies.

Historians have written that America's second president, John Adams, was changed from a passive, hesitant man to a strong-willed political leader by the influence of his wife, Abigail. When Adams attended the first Continental Congress in 1774, Abigail wrote him daily offering her advice. During her husband's one term as president (1797-1801), Abigail often stood in as his representative at official government functions, even frequently reviewing and inspecting the military. Abigail, who never doubted that women were men's intellectual equals, was attacked by her husband's political foes, who insisted upon calling her "Mrs. President," in an attempt to embarrass the administration. John Adams himself often commented that his wife was the one person in whom he could trust and openly confide.

When Woodrow Wilson suffered a stroke near the end of his presidency (1913-1921), his wife, Edith, secretly carried out many of his presidential duties. Wilson earlier had taught her the top-secret diplomatic code used during World War I, something that even his Secretary of State did not know.

But perhaps the most influential first lady, before Hillary, was Eleanor Roosevelt, the wife of Franklin

Delano Roosevelt. Franklin had been stricken with crippling polio before becoming president, and during his long tenure as Chief Executive (1933-1945) Eleanor often served, in her husband's expression, as his "legs, eyes and ears." Perceived as more progressive than Franklin, she was often criticized for pushing her husband toward liberal positions. In addition to her role as advisor to her husband, Eleanor wrote a newspaper column entitled "My Day," and broadcast her views regularly on the radio. When Franklin died, early into his fourth term, she was called the "First Lady of the World." President Harry Truman, who succeeded Franklin Roosevelt, appointed her as a delegate to the new United Nations in 1946, where she served as the first chairperson of the United Nation's Commission on Human Rights.

Many other first ladies have had a powerful influence on their husbands. Rosalyn Carter, President Jimmy Carter's wife, created controversy by attending Cabinet meetings. Nancy Reagan was occasionally overheard prompting President Ronald Reagan's answers to reporter's questions.

But it is clear that Hillary and Bill are planning to take her role to a new level of public involvement, and it is far too early to judge their success.

In the midst of all the excitement of becoming first lady, sadness occurred in Hillary's life. Her father, Hugh Rodham Sr., died on April 9, 1993, at age 81. Although Hugh was a life-long Republican, he had told the press he had "found it in his heart" to vote for his son-in-law. Hillary has spoken about her deep love and appreciation for her father. When Hugh suffered the first of a series of final strokes and was hospitalized, Hillary canceled her busy schedule to comfort him by his hospital bed.

Both Hillary and Bill have spoken of the difficulty they have finding family time in their busy schedules. Hillary assumes most of the child rearing responsibilities. When Chelsea arrives home from school, usually after soccer or softball practice, Hillary walks from her office to the East Wing to spend a few minutes with her daughter. When school is canceled because of snow, Hillary sometimes takes the day off to watch videos or play cards with Chelsea. Hillary and Bill divide the homework help they provide for Chelsea. Bill is responsible for helping with math. Chelsea does her homework in the small study next to the Oval Office, so she can ask him math questions. Hillary often provides help with essays and book reviews.

Togetherness continues with the 7 p.m. dinner

hour. When both Bill and Hillary are in Washington, they insist their schedules be cleared so the family can enjoy a meal together, and discuss the day's events. Clearly, the Clintons are trying to make the White House a real home.

Great challenges face the first family, and the nation; no one can know what changes the future holds. One change is already certain—Hillary Rodham Clinton has made it easier for women to dream of holding high public office. That is no small accomplishment, but it comes as no surprise to anyone aware of Hillary's life of achievement.

For Further Reading

Allen, Charles F., *The Comeback Kid: The Life And Career Of Bill Clinton*, Birch Lane Press: New York, 1992.

Germond, Jack and Jules Witcover, *Mad As Hell: Revolt At The Ballot Box, 1992*, Warner Books: New York, 1993.

King, Norman, *Hillary: Her True Story*, Birch Lane Press: New York, 1993.

Levin, Robert E., *Bill Clinton: The Inside Story*, S.P.I. Books: New York, 1992.

Martin, Gene L. and Aaron Boyd, *Bill Clinton: President From Arkansas*, Tudor Publishers: Greensboro, NC, 1993.

Radcliffe, Donnie, *Hillary Rodham Clinton: A First Lady For Our Time*, Warner Books: New York, 1993.

Warner, Judith, *Hillary Clinton: The Inside Story*, New American Library: New York, 1993.

Index

92
CLI

Boyd, Aaron.

First lady.

$17.95

DATE			

HAROLD C. UREY MIDDLE SCHOOL

BAKER & TAYLOR BOOKS